KARMA COUPLES

A Spiritual Self-Help Guide for Troubled Karmic Relationships

Academy of Spiritual Practice

MICHELLE ROBINSON
Bach. Counseling, Dip. Clinical Hypnosis, B.A. Dip. Ed.

KARMA COUPLES

A Spiritual Self-Help Guide for Troubled Karmic Relationships

Academy of Spiritual Practice

MICHELLE ROBINSON
Bach. Counseling, Dip. Clinical Hypnosis, B.A. Dip. Ed.

Mind Potential Publishing
by *The Potentialist*

Copyright © 2021 Michelle Robinson and the Academy of Spiritual Practice.

ALL RIGHTS RESERVED. No part of this book may be reproduced or transmitted in any form whatsoever, electronic, or mechanical, including photocopying, recording, or by any informational storage or retrieval system without the expressed written permission from the author and publisher.

Author: Michelle Robinson
Title: Karma Couples
ISBN Paperback: 978-1-922380-39-5
ISBN Kindle: 978-1-922380-41-8

 A catalogue record for this book is available from the National Library of Australia

Category: Self Help Techniques | Mind and Body

Publisher: Mind Potential Publishing
Division of Mind Design Centre Pty Ltd,
PO Box 6094, Maroochydore BC
Queensland, Australia, 4558.
International Phone: +61 405 138 567
Australia Phone: 1300 664 544
Publisher: www.mindpotentialpublishing.com

Author: www.trustyourintuition.com
www.academyofspiritualpractice.com

Cover design by: www.ngirldesign.com.au

LIMITS OF LIABILITY | DISCLAIMER OF WARRANTY: The author and publisher of this book have used their best efforts in preparing this material and they disclaim any warranties, (expressed or implied) for any particular purpose. The information presented in this publication is compiled from sources believed to be accurate at the time of printing, however the publisher assumes no responsibility for omissions or errors.

The author and publisher shall not be held liable for any loss or other damages, including, but not limited to incidental, consequential, or any other. This publication is not intended to replace or substitute medical or professional advice, the author and publisher disclaim any liability, loss or risk incurred as a direct or indirect consequence of the use of any content.

Mind Potential Publishing bears no responsibility for the accuracy of the information provided as either online or offline links contained in this publication. The use of links to websites does not constitute an endorsement by the publisher. The publisher assumes no liability for content or opinion expressed by the author. Opinions expressed by the Author do not represent the opinion of Mind Potential Publishing nor their subsidiaries.

Mind Potential Publishing bears no responsibility for the accuracy of the information provided in online or offline links contained in this publication. The use of links to websites does not constitute an endorsement by the publisher. The publisher assumes no liability for content or opinion expressed by the author.

Printed in Australia

CONTENTS

How To Gain the Most from this Book	1
Foreword	3
Sunflowers and Destiny	5
Lesson 1: Recognize Your Signposts	9
Lesson 2: All the World's A Stage	23
Lesson 3: Make Peace with the Toad in Your Head	33
Lesson 4: Never Let Someone Else Become Your Oxygen	41
Lesson 5: When Love Is a Shipwreck, Always Rebuild On Dry Ground	47
Lesson 6: Ignore the Doomsayers. Audit Your Friends' Advice	57
Lesson 7: Leave the Past in The Past	65
Lesson 8: Weeds are Just Overachievers. Learn to Love Them The Aspects of Love	75
Lesson 9: Gratitude is the First Aspect of Love	85
Lesson 10: Honor is the Second Aspect of Love	91
Lesson 11: Compassion is the Third Aspect of Love	97
Lesson 12: Forgiveness is the Fourth Aspect of Love	103
Lesson 13: Truth is the Final Aspect of Love	109
Epilogue	115
Love on the Other Side. Personal Responses to Frequently Asked Questions	117
Acknowledgements	134
Testimonials	135
Meet the Author	137
Other Books, Courses and Products by Michelle Robinson	140

HOW TO GAIN THE MOST FROM THIS BOOK

Karma Couples guides you through a process of evaluating your relationship with your partner so that you develop clarity and a deeper understanding of the karmic lessons in this relationship.

Some of the activities in this book include a meditation. I have explained each meditation carefully so that you have the option to record it on your phone, and listen to your own voice, if you choose.

> You can also download (or play online) the complimentary MP3 audios of the *Karma Couples* meditations that I have recorded from the following website address: **www.bit.ly/karmacouples**

- Please always listen with headphones, in a quiet place where you will be undisturbed.
- Recording your insights as you move through the chapters is helpful for later reflection.

FOREWORD

I have to be honest and say this isn't a book about how to find love.

It isn't the next instalment in cosmic attraction theory and neither does it pretend to be a guide to the perfect relationship for perfect partners.

However, it is a romance. It will teach you how to love, not in the small singular way where someone is right and someone is wrong, but in the grand expansive way where it does not matter who did what, when, or who did not do the right thing then, because you can let it all go and move on.

It is a book about pulling those prickles of resentment and guilt out of your backside and finally being able to sit peacefully with yourself. It will help you realize that too many people are hurt by your hanging on to pain and not the least of these people is yourself. Your **true** self.

Mainly, it is a book about coming out of the frozen sleep in which you believe the dramas of your life are real, and waking to the lessons behind the events, the love behind the hurts, and the opportunities for forgiveness waiting for you like unopened gifts.

None of it is easy. All of it is beautiful. Of that, you are the ultimate judge.

FOREWORD

All insights offered are my own and are not intended to offend or replace any spiritual beliefs you may hold. I respect faith in its many expressions. Hold true to what feels right for you.

Likewise, the responses in the section *Love On the Other Side*, are my own, and developed after many years of spiritual reading, conducting past-life regressions (in which I am qualified) and talking with people during my years in spiritual ministry. They are my opinions only and should not be accepted as proven facts. Until each of us passes into the world that meets us when we die, we cannot know the full truth of what awaits.

SUNFLOWERS AND DESTINY

Inspiration from Spirit:

Do not be afraid, for all that comes has already gone before you. The tides of life must flow, and to wish otherwise blocks the cycle of renewal to which you belong.

It was an overcast morning and heavy with Summer's humid breath. Birds sang with what energy they could still muster by 8 am, and there was the promise of an afternoon storm.

I had never felt so afraid.

A cough sounded from the bedroom and the man of my dreams emerged - the man of my broken dreams whose bed I had sworn I would never share again. We were ex-partners, ex-lovers and exited from relationship, or so I had told myself. Yet here I was, in his house and about as far out on a limb as any petrified animal could crawl.

Thoughts like, *"What on earth were you thinking?"* and *"Girl, you should run for your life!"* tumbled through my mind. I felt helpless and terrified at the same time. One theme drew these threads together and coursed through me like a stream.

"I can't go through this again!"

It was then, as I looked out of the living room window, I saw it. One lonely sunflower, straggly and untended, grew on a patch of earth across the street. It stared at me in a silent challenge, urging me to wake up and recognise its signal.

And I did. My mind flashed back ten years to my first morning in a rented home after leaving my husband. That was another hot, sticky day, and with teenagers squabbling in the kitchen and the burden of a failed marriage on my conscience,

I stepped into the front yard to catch a breeze. I'm not ashamed to admit I was crying. I had never felt so confused and sad. I had entered my marriage with the confidence our love would last a lifetime, but petty struggles had become major wars and the damage was enormous.

Keen to distance my tears from the kids, I walked towards an overgrown garden bed. It was a mess of weeds and thorns yet standing defiantly among the chaos was a single sunflower, fully in bloom, straining its heavy head towards the sky. The symbolism of its beauty and courage was not lost on me. Despite its surroundings, the sunflower just stood its ground, lifting its face to the sky, being the best, it could be. I smiled through my tears in gratitude for its courage and its lesson. From that moment on, sunflowers became my personal emblem for endurance and faith.

Back in the present, it was as if a switch had turned on and I knew everything was going to be okay. Not okay in that glib, easy way of pretending that a painful past has never occurred. I'm not that naive, nor at forty-eight, was I that young. However, as I turned to see my companion calmly putting on the jug to make a cup of tea, and then turned again to look at the sunflower, something in me acknowledged the significance of the moment.

Everything had led us to this. The fading flush of first love, the loss and pain of separation, the coming together again, more than once, that was smashed by more pain and more separation - all these experiences led us here.

I paused, feeling strangely calm after the recent moments of fear. Could I really trust my emotional survival to a sunflower?

> **Was my inner guidance calling me to be courageous one more time?**

"Are you ready for breakfast?" I heard him ask with a newly found tenderness.

"Yes," I replied. "But first you need to know why. Come to the window. I have something to share with you."

And so, our real journey together began.

LESSON 1
RECOGNIZE YOUR SIGNPOSTS

Inspiration from Spirit:

Some minds sleep for many lifetimes, but it is always their destiny to return home to the Womb of the Source and finally be awakened to their Light.

It may seem strange to begin a book about love with an anecdote featuring a sunflower and a decision that could have been a crazy risk.

Actually, there were two signs in that twenty-four-hour period indicating that my partner and I had turned an indefinable corner and were ready to recommit to a relationship.

The sunflower was the second sign, occurring the morning after we spent the night together. How I had ended up staying the night also hinged on a sign.

It wasn't the fact he had told me he was ready to spend the rest of his life with me, although he had. I had listened to his words wearing my invisible raincoat because I was too afraid to let them penetrate. I had heard words like that before.

RECOGNIZE YOUR SIGNPOSTS

It was the tone of voice with which he spoke to my dog.

Although we had remained close friends since our most recent separation, I drew the line at spending the night together. I was too fragile, too broken to survive the kickback a temporary fling would offer. We'd tried it and I'd already paid the price.

So, after a very pleasant meal at his home, I casually told my dog to join me at the car. Sally is a rescue-dog who often accompanies me on outings. Being in her older years, she was in no hurry to move and I found myself there without her.

Then I heard a voice. *"Come on, Darling,"* he said to Sally. *"Mum's waiting for you."*

He spoke softly and kindly, not for my ears, because I was some distance away. His voice floated over me as I stood with my hand on the doorhandle.

I can't tell you what happened next because there are no words to describe it. Some shift in energy, some kind of recognition stirred in me. He was no lover of dogs and the man I had committed to and lost would never have called Sally, 'Darling.'

I turned to face him, searching for the words to fit my confusion. The best I could manage was to point out the obvious.

"You just called Sally, Darling," I said incredulously.

"That's right," he smiled. *"You're my first Darling and she's my Darling as well. Do you have a problem with that?"*

I let that sink into me for a while. No, I decided, I didn't. In fact, I didn't have a problem at all.

"It's okay," I replied. *"Leave her where she is. I've decided I can stay."*

Obviously, it would be irresponsible to advocate staying in a broken relationship based on the way your partner talks to your dog or because you saw a sunflower growing across the street.

> *What I am saying is that our inner guidance offers us signposts or signals if we are open to recognizing them.*

These are our wake-up calls, the subtle reminders that something significant is occurring. Our inner guidance whispers, *"Slow down. Take notice."*

Sometimes these signals present as events of synchronicity. We might think, *"What were the chances of that?"* Excuse the pun, but chances are it was not chance.

> *Once you begin to consciously tune into your life, taking the time to be aware of how you feel about people, places, and events, you will realize that your inner guidance speaks with you, often.*

You will become aware that you have a relationship with Divinity, (with the Source, the Universe, your Higher Self, God, the Divine Spirit or whatever name you prefer), and with a range of spiritual beings who are helping you experience the lessons you came to Earth to learn.

These spiritual beings are our loved ones, guides, angels and teachers who, with the speed of thought, draw close to support us. It helps if we ask for their assistance but whether we know it or not they send us healing energy, love and practical help.

In order to communicate with us they use many different channels, including our intuition, our dreams, meditation, prayer, and even our sense of 'knowing' what feels right. All this information contributes to our inner guidance. It gently leads us towards healthy, positive decisions and gives us courage when we fall or feel we have failed.

It is important to remember that our spiritual guides encourage us; they do not control us or enforce their will. We are responsible for the decisions we make and the paths we choose. That's what freewill is all about.

> *We are responsible for the decisions we make and the paths we choose. That's what freewill is all about.*

However, we are never unloved or alone.

The hard part is that while our spiritual friends see and hear us, our perspective is limited by our immediate environment.

If you find this hard to imagine, picture yourself sitting at the edge of a pond. You can see into the pond and observe small fish swimming below the surface. It is easy for you to watch them as they interact and forage for food. However, the fish cannot turn their heads upwards to see you. Unless you cast your shadow over their pond or put your hand into the water, you simply do not exist in their dimension.

Just as these fish that cannot see us, most of us cannot routinely see into the spiritual world. Events we cannot explain may seem like miracles; usually, however, it is our spiritual guidance at work.

Think about this carefully. Many of the signposts you will encounter during your life are markers you set while you were still in the spirit world. You will recognize these markers by an inner awareness, a knowing that something has just 'woken up' inside you, as I did when I saw the sunflower across the street and heard the tone of my partner's voice.

Much earlier in my life, I had recognized my first husband the moment our eyes met. It was the acknowledgement of a karmic contract even though back then I did not know what karma was. In just a glance between us on a crowded plane, I felt an exclamation mark in my energy field. In that brief contact, two souls recognized each other. It was different from sexual attraction and neither one of us was looking for a relationship, yet, within two months I told my mother I'd met the father of my children.

Perhaps you can now reflect on similar incidents. Have you felt you have lived particular moments before? Have you ever looked into someone's eyes and recognized them immediately? Have you chosen to love someone for reasons even you could not fathom? Have you just *known* you had to make a certain decision because you were compelled to do it?

If so, you may already be following the invisible signposts you anchored on your timeline or the subtle messages of your spiritual friends.

With so much guidance available, you may wonder why relationships are so confusing.

Well, as the saying goes, "This is your life." And guess what? You chose it.

Do You Have An Intuitive Gift?

Receive your free intuitive gifts guidebook …

Discover the 7 Signs It's Your Destiny To Work With Your Intuitive Gifts'.

**Download a free
Intuitive Gifts Destiny Guidebook at**
www.yourintuitivegiftsatwork.com/destinyguide

If you are aware of synchronicity or receive signals from the Universe and Spirit, you have an intuitive gift.

Your soul may even be calling you to develop and work with your gifts to help others.

This guide will help you get clarity about whether your intuitive gifts are already working for you.

Request your free guidebook here and it will be emailed to you immediately:
www.yourintuitivegiftsatwork.com/destinyguide

Need Support? Join My Free Facebook Group
You may also like to join my free Facebook group where I offer tips and helpful information about developing your gifts and other spiritual topics. You can join – no costs involved – here:

www.facebook.com/groups/yourintuitivegiftsatwork

Activity

This exercise will help you connect with your inner guidance.

- Inner guidance refers to information from a variety of sources. The different sources merge like tributaries joining a stream. Sometimes we don't know exactly how the information comes together, but we receive a stream of guidance that provides insights when we need them.

- The channel that carries this inner guidance is often our imagination. Learning to trust information when it feels like we are 'making it up' is important. With

RECOGNIZE YOUR SIGNPOSTS

practice, you will be able to discern the difference between pure imagination, and spiritual messages.

- Spiritual messages often come in the form of symbols, so you need to establish a language everyone understands.

- Shortly after my close friend died, I asked her for a symbol that would prove she had heard me talking with her. In my mind I saw a white dove. I affirmed that I would look for a white dove in the immediate future as confirmation she had sent this image.

- In the next two days, I saw three white doves, all in unusual circumstances. I knew my friend and I had made contact, and my heart felt lighter. She had known in advance that the white dove would cross my path in several ways, and so the symbol was meaningful and timely.

- In addition to a friend in spirit sending you symbols; you can choose symbols for your spiritual helpers to use when communicating with you. These symbols provide guidance when you have a question.

Sit quietly and choose just a few images that have a specific meaning for you. Keep your symbols simple and direct.

Let your spiritual helpers know the messages these symbols will hold for you. Eventually, symbols will come into your mind or manifest in your life in response to your questions.

> Relationships are always evolving, so be open to receiving new symbols as you communicate.
>
> With practice, you can use symbolic language to receive guidance during meditation. Here is a straightforward example. My symbol for, "Be careful," is a yellow traffic light. If I received that symbol when considering a new job offer, I would make sure I did more research before I accepted that position.

Keep your symbols simple, direct, and available in the physical world. Draw or write your symbols in a journal. This is the beginning of a rich language that will continue to evolve.

Your spiritual helpers can hear your thoughts any time you choose; however, it will be easier for you to receive their messages if you are peaceful. Meditation is an excellent means of achieving a peaceful state of mind.

Preparing for Meditation

In meditation your energy is as close as it can be to the higher vibration of the spirit world. This is the ideal time to communicate with your spiritual friends or guides.

- Sit or lie in a comfortable position. Focus your attention on your breath and feel yourself relaxing.

Visualize your heart center opening as your inner light expands and shines brightly.

- Connect with the brilliant White Light of the Source (God, the Divine Spirit or whatever name you prefer). Feel the Light entering the crown of your head, pouring through you and out the soles of your feet.

- See or imagine this White Light flooding your entire environment. Say to yourself, "*The Light protects me. The Light surrounds me. I am Light.*"

- Let your inner light and the Light from the Source merge to become one.

- Allow yourself to relax. Scan your body, gently releasing each muscle in turn. Breathe the White Light down into your abdomen and relax deeper as you exhale.

- When you feel ready, mentally ask to connect with the spirit world.

You may feel some tingling around your face, neck and hair or a subtle ripple in your energy field. You may feel a gentle, warm pressure touching a hand. Your spiritual helpers will try to let you know they are with you in loving, non-invasive ways, so do not be afraid. They only blend with your energy-field and thoughts; they never enter your physical body. It is mind to mind communication.

Should you ever feel uncomfortable, ask them to retreat so their vibration feels less intense. This is unlikely to happen, but it is useful to know you have this ability.

Your spiritual friends will not intentionally alarm or frighten you; however, a loved one may be excited to make contact and their vibration may surprise you.

Please understand that many people communicate through thoughts alone, and do not feel changes in vibration. This communication is equally valid and real.

Meditation - Connection

Step 1	Once you are relaxed, ask to connect with the person you want to hear from; say their name and visualize them clearly.
	If you hold an item they owned or a photo, this may enhance the connection. The strongest connections between our worlds come from love and need.
	Needs will differ depending on the relationship. Sometimes the need is to express gratitude, and other times, it may be to apologize. For example, a daughter may need reassurance that her mother is well and healed in the spirit world, and an adult child in the spirit world may need to apologize to their family for the pain caused when they took their own life. The energy that accompanies a heart-felt need for healing is powerful.

RECOGNIZE YOUR SIGNPOSTS

Step 2	If you wish to communicate with your teaching guides, request that connection.

It is also natural to ask for spiritual assistance from those who watch over you, without specifying their identities. You have a team of spiritual helpers working with you throughout your life. On any occasion, you want the best spiritual guidance possible. |
| **Step 3** | After choosing with whom you will connect, request that they send you a mental picture of something you will come across in the next few days.

This symbol will be straightforward so that you can recognize it when you see it. When you receive an image or even a word, record it in your journal and wait for it to manifest. |
| **Step 4** | Next, respectfully share with Spirit the symbols you have chosen and their meanings. Do this by visualizing each image and sending clear thoughts about what it means.

It is best to build your language slowly so that each symbol is firmly understood before adding a new one.

This communication allows you to speak to your spiritual guidance, including your own intuition, any time you choose. The symbols you receive in response to your questions will help clarify your issue or problem |

Step 5	When you have completed sharing your symbols, remember to give thanks and bring your attention back to the present moment. Stretch, and make sure you are completely grounded and alert before you stand or resume usual activities.

Opportunity to Further Develop Your Gifts

If you know you have an intuitive gift and would like to develop it further, you might like to purchase my book, which is a great text for developing excellence when using your intuitive gifts. You can find out more here:

www.yourintuitivegiftsatwork.com/book
or to purchase the book from my website:
www.trustyourintuition.com/shop-now

LESSON 2
ALL THE WORLD'S A STAGE

Inspiration from Spirit:

All spirits who come into human form feel abandoned. You are disappointed by those with whom you form relationships, yet how could it be otherwise? Contracts are not easy to discern, and a pain-free path may not be the life you have chosen. Those who you feel have hurt you may be your wisest teachers and your closest friends.

Here is a statement I think you will agree with. It is hard to be spiritually loving and forgiving when you feel someone has betrayed you. It doesn't matter how rational and compassionate you are, when the person you love betrays you or leaves you, or even if you have betrayed them, life hurts.

Given I have woven a rich tapestry in my life, I have endured many sleepless nights wondering why past relationships failed. I have spent months rehashing events and looking for clues to explain why I kept finding myself on the same roundabout with another broken heart. During most of that time, I did not like the person I had become. I felt mean, unloving and hateful towards those I believed had hurt me and also towards myself.

What saved me from this nightmare was finally understanding a simple lesson:

I am the architect and creator of my life.

Your lesson is that you are the architect and creator of yours. It seems incredible, but it is true.

Whether or not you are consciously aware of it, a deeper part of you knows that you are much more than a human body. In the same way that you have felt guided at significant moments in your life, you will know that you existed long before you came to Earth and you will exist long after you leave at death.

> *The real 'you' is a spiritual being housed within the vessel of your soul. This soul incarnates many times and your evolution is assured. You cannot fail.*

You are a spark or child of the Divine Source, and your time on Earth allows you countless opportunities to evolve. The purpose of coming into physical life is to grow in love. Ultimately, since the Source is pure love, each of us is following the path back home. In order to become more loving, we seek lessons and experiences that test us so we can master what we need to work on.

When we are in the spirit world, we do not have these opportunities to the same degree as when we are on Earth, because in spirit we have greater knowledge available. To really discover if we have mastered our lessons, we need to be challenged in practical situations where all we can draw on is our inner guidance and faith.

It is a little like leaving home to face an exam. It was our choice to undertake the study, and we know we should be okay because we have done the learning elsewhere. However, in this practical exam, we have to apply our knowledge in new situations. There are no textbooks allowed. Sometimes we become distracted and forget what we have learned, or we get a challenging question and our learning flies out the window. Know the feeling? This simple analogy is rather like what happens to us on Earth.

We choose to incarnate with gratitude. A human life is always a gift, and spiritually we know this.

However, coming to Earth also takes courage, because we do not consciously remember who we are and why we are here. We will lose people we love, experience pain and eventually face our own physical death; nothing is surer.

We will have joyous times and sad times. We will feel strong and invincible and at other times, weak and vulnerable. There are no right or wrong experiences. Every experience is an opportunity to grow. To make the most of our experiences, we need to connect with our inner compass and listen to the guidance that is offered.

You are the architect and creator of your life because before you incarnated, you chose the major events and relationships you would encounter.

We all did, and we always do. This process is undertaken with the help of our spiritual guides who, like us, understand the lessons we need to learn.

A life on Earth inevitably involves challenges as well as pleasure, suffering as well as joy. This provides us with a stage on which we can exercise decision making and freewill.

> *We are actors in a play that we agreed to, at least in draft form, before we came back.*

Since we never truly die, the stakes are not as high as they seem, and our Earthly amnesia is a blessing. How could we fully engage with our current life if we were haunted by our lives in the past?

Once we are born, we shape how the play unfolds according to a wide range of possibilities available to us, and every decision activates a range of probabilities in response.

To help us out, other souls volunteer to act in the roles of those we love, hate, envy, admire, marry, divorce and so on. They want us to have the best opportunities to grow, and in return we assist them.

These spiritual contracts allow us to develop the qualities we need. These qualities are all aspects of the Divine Source. They are all aspects of love.

Through experiencing a divorce, we might learn inner strength and ultimately forgiveness. Through surviving a loved one's death, we might develop resilience and compassion. Through experiencing betrayal, we might finally fight for our self-worth and integrity.

In the karmic tapestry of many lifetimes, we perform a wide range of roles as heroes and villains, helpers and victims, lovers, and betrayers of trust.

Let me be clear about one thing, however. There is no excuse for abuse and no praise for cruelty. We choose through our freewill *how* we fulfil our spiritual contracts, and these are always designed to benefit others. If we step outside our agreed role and inflict harm because we are blinded by power, greed or self-importance, we will incur karmic debt and lose opportunities to grow.

More importantly, our spiritual helpers never wish us to stay in an abusive or harmful relationship. What they do want is for us to remember why we are here. They want us to become conscious of the relationship patterns we are sustaining so that we recognize the lessons we chose to learn. If senseless pain is the fabric of our relationship, it is okay to move on. If the karmic contract has been fulfilled or even forgotten, it is still okay to move on. There is nothing to be gained by clinging to hurtful, constricting or soul-numbing relationships.

> *The fragile you in this soul-expression is just one facet of a beautiful diamond, one aspect of your inner light which has shined for an eternity. Your failure is not a possibility.*

It does not matter how far you have strayed from your karmic blueprint or how many signposts you have missed this time around; your spiritual helpers never give up on you. Every moment is an opportunity to create, and you can choose to create relationships that are worthy of you.

Your current lesson is to recognise that the people who have hurt you are most likely your spiritual friends, merely acting their agreed roles. Their mandate may be to shake you out of your complacency and bring you to this point, where to survive you must remember who you are.

Without denying or minimizing your pain, reflect now on the flip side of your experiences. No matter how confused or angry you feel, take stock of what you have gained. What strengths have been forged that you can call on in the future? What have you learned about discernment? About choosing more carefully who to trust? What greater contribution can you make to your life and the lives of others because you have learned to stand up for your truth?

If it is too soon and you are too raw to acknowledge your resilience, then for now just allow yourself some hope. Allow yourself to believe that with the Divinity within you, positive change is possible.

If you can soften some of your pain and admit that you have grown, however begrudgingly, you have taken the first step to healing. This is true whether you are contemplating rebuilding a relationship or have decided to move on.

The next step is to make peace with the toad in your head. You need to make peace with yourself.

Activity

> This exercise allows you to reflect on your current relationship from a spiritual perspective. If you would like to record your answers, first write the questions in your journal.
>
> Sit or lie in a place where you will not be disturbed. Quieten your mind and focus on your breath as you relax. If thoughts from the day intrude, imagine them as leaves falling gently from a tree. Do not try to stop them or hold them. Observe them and let them go.
>
> Become aware of the light in the center of your heart and visualize this light expanding, shining brightly. As you take some deeper, slow breaths, imagine this light filling your body.
>
> Ask that your inner guidance responds to the following questions. Remain in your calm state and let the answers flow. Do not judge or hinder them.

Is my relationship with (insert name) a soul contract we made before coming to Earth?

If the answer is 'yes,' ask:

1	Is (insert name) a member of my soul group? (You can also use the term soul family if you prefer.)
2	What lessons or experiences did I hope to gain through this contract?
3	What lessons or experiences did (insert name) hope to gain through this contract? "Are we on track in this relationship from a spiritual perspective? Why or why not?"
4	Is this relationship honoring me? Is this relationship damaging me?
5	Are we done yet, or is there more to experience and learn?

If you do not feel there is a soul contract, ask:

1	Is this relationship honoring me?
2	Is this relationship damaging me?
3	What strengths or lessons have I gained from this relationship?
4	Are we done yet, or is there more to experience and learn?

Listen carefully to the answers that flow from your heart. When you have completed this exercise, reflect on the information.

What insights have you gained about soul contracts with your partner? This activity helps you to understand any close relationship in your life.

_____
_____
_____
_____

LESSON 3

MAKE PEACE WITH THE TOAD IN YOUR HEAD

Inspiration from Spirit:

The way to move past your illusions and fears is to recognize them. The monsters that toss restlessly in your subconscious mind have grotesque faces, but they are all your own creations.

I did not know I had a toad in my head until about three years ago. I was deep in meditation, listening for the first time to another one of those audios claiming to enhance my spiritual mastery, when the hypnotic voice asked me to search beneath the layers of my conscious mind and see what I discovered.

Nothing could have prepared me for the image that presented itself.

There, flattened and hiding under all my layers of respectability and professionalism, was a *toad*!

It seemed to be panting, as toads do when they are discovered and stressed. I recoiled in horror.

"What are you?" I asked over and over again. "Why are you in my head?"

The toad was huge, furtive and very afraid. It felt like it had been chased by too many brooms, scalded with too much cruelty and in all its ugliness, it cried out for compassion.

My first instinct was to get rid of it, now!

I visualized pouring salt on its back as if a spiritual cleansing could clear it. It didn't work. The toad just looked more miserable and clung to the space in my head with all its might. Cowering. Dejected. Ashamed.

For days, I could think of nothing else. I affirmed it "Gone!" I prayed it would be taken from me, like a negative energetic intruder, but the toad held its ground.

I walked and prayed and thought, and finally realized that the toad represented all the parts of me I had suppressed and hidden during my life. It was the guilt I had retained from my failed marriage, and the pain of twelve years of child sexual abuse. It was all the criticisms I had believed about myself and the cruelty of unjust judgments. That toad was part of me and ultimately, I had to befriend it.

I put a pink bow on its poor bald head and stopped trying to persecute it. Believe me; it had been persecuted enough.

It is my theory that we all have some kind of 'toad' in our heads.

Although we are Divine beings, we take on too much unhelpful 'baggage' in our relationships.

We smile away or shrug off the hurtful jibes of parents, lovers, children and so-called friends, but the problem is, there's no 'away' or 'off' about it. Deep down we are too ready to believe that we are stupid, lazy, fat, crazy, or any other dark adjective that has been slung at us because of someone else's frustration.

Deep down, we crave to be approved of and loved, and when that does not happen, the hurt, scared and ashamed parts of us run for cover and dig deep.
They evade discovery until we stumble across them by turning on a light in the darkest corners of our being.

The most important lesson I learned is that directing hate and blame at something that already feels hated and ashamed will never work. There is no healing in that.

I cannot unmake my past. I cannot take back the pain my failed marriage caused. I cannot undo the sexual abuse. I cannot kill the toad.

And yet ...

- I *can* decide to come to a place of peace with it.

- *I can* feel compassion for the parts of me that have been hurt and broken.

- *I can*, without denying personal responsibility, forgive myself for mistakes I made in the past.

- *I can* free myself from the need to seek approval from others.

- *I can* allow these gifts of kindness to myself because from this point forward, I can choose to do things differently.

And so can you.
It is hard being blind in the world of form, sightless to the spiritual purpose that guides us.

> *We forget that we are doing the best we can in a life whose instructions are in Braille. We forget that while we are here experiencing 'humanness', we are actually eternal, lovable and much-loved souls.*

We worry about our weight, our looks, our possessions, our jobs, when none of these things matter for one second the moment we take our last breath and cross into the spirit world. Once in our spiritual home, we remember the contracts we made and who we really are. We become the judges of our lives, and this process of review is supported by loving spiritual guides.

We are able to see what we did well, what lessons we accomplished and the lessons we still have to learn. We see the totality of our life and feel the consequences of our actions from the perspectives of all the people we interacted with - the good and the bad. We see the karma we have created and what we will have to address in the future to regain spiritual balance. However, we are kind to ourselves and know we have more chances to grow next time around.

Developing this insight during an Earthly life is a wonderful gift. Suddenly we have the freedom to see our relationships differently.

We are able to accept all parts of ourselves and choose now to embrace who we will become.

We can make honest, lasting peace, with the toad.

Activity

The following exercise will release energy blocks and belief patterns that limit the real you.

As children and as adults, we unknowingly absorb comments, opinions and criticisms from significant people in our lives. Many of these comments are judgments which reduce our confidence and stop us being who we truly are. They take root in our energy field without us even realizing they are there.

The following affirmation statements release fear, the need for approval and guilt. Use them, and also write your own affirmation statements to clear any other unhelpful blocks you sense. Repeat them often and you will notice a positive difference in your confidence and expression.

Personalize the statements to make the release as powerful as possible.

For Releasing Fear

In all lives, past, present, and future, I destroy all blocks, beliefs and conditioning that prevent me from knowing I am safe and have always been safe. I am an eternal soul who cannot die. I release fearful energy, returning it to the Source for healing. So be it and so it is.

For Releasing the Need for Other People's Approval

In all lives, past, present, and future, where I have limited myself in order to gain another person's love and approval, I release this energy and send it to the Source for healing. I am who I am and that is enough. I am who I am and that's okay. So be it and so it is.

For Releasing Guilt and Shame

In all lives, past, present, and future, I release all energy that has trapped me into believing I am unworthy of love, undeserving of happiness and deserving of shame. The pain of my past leaves me now. Enough is enough. So be it and so it is.

Do this when you have some private time and send the unwanted energy back to the Source for healing. Releasing the conditioning and the heavy mantel of other people's expectations will make you feel lighter and free. Better still, you will finally have the confidence to do your soul's work in this incarnation.

LESSON 4
NEVER LET SOMEONE ELSE BECOME YOUR OXYGEN

Inspiration from Spirit:

When you accept your own true nature and cease looking for yourself in others, the love you no longer need will come to you. Seek first the true self within, for you must have a reflection that is your own when you are drawn to a mirror.

This lesson cannot be emphasized too strongly.

Never make another person responsible for your life.

Needing a partner because we cannot exist without them is so close to the antithesis of love that it is hard to think of a better example of what love is not. It is a huge misuse of our responsibilities and freewill to expect another person to give us our reasons to live.

We are strong, resilient souls who came to Earth for reasons that differ from those of our partners. A karmic contract may have been negotiated to help us develop qualities we lack, but a contract does not absolve us from the personal responsibility for our life.

At a human level, most people have a standard response to a partner who is needy; they run for their lives.

It was a lesson I learned when I was dying of a broken heart.

When I first separated from my partner, I did not think I could survive it. I felt like I could not breathe, like the air did not have enough oxygen anymore. Every afternoon after work, for at least six weeks, I was crippled with anxiety. My first instinct was to phone him, and I did. He answered, but always sounded fine. He missed me, but his life was continuing. Mine was a shamble of angular hurts and fears that distressed me day and night.

During our three-year relationship I had become close friends with his work colleagues. We partied often and hard, enjoying a social life that unintentionally excluded my friends. I was swept up in the heady delights of dinners at restaurants and parties at the home we had bought together.

When our relationship ended, it was natural that the majority of our friends continued to socialize with him. We sold our home and I moved into a small rental property, which was located, ironically, on *Paradise Street*. During the following months I was blessed with a few physical angels who rescued me from my dejection, even providing me with a bed on nights I could not cope. I felt awful all the time, as if I was dying inside. However, I was also determined to live.

As the weeks went on, I began to re-weave the tapestry of my life. I found a development circle and a spiritual church in my area. Prior to meeting my partner, I had been heavily involved in spirituality, and so I reconnected with like-minded people and made new friends.

My partner and I came back together after about six months, only to part again, before we finally stabilized our relationship. However, I never went through the same agony of suffocation as I did the first time. I had learned how to take responsibility for my oxygen and my life. Once that happened, I was apparently much more attractive as a life-partner. In fact, I was the *only* life-partner he wanted. I would never have predicted that.

The point of this lesson is that true love does not reduce or diminish our expression of whom we are.

> **A positive partnership will make you more when you are together and not less when you are alone.**

This brings us to the next lesson - how to survive a relationship shipwreck.

Activity

This exercise allows you to reflect on issues of power and control in your relationships.

- Sit quietly and connect to your inner light and the White Light of the Source.

- Reflect on whether there is a harmonious balance of power in the key relationships in your life.

- If one person is needy or controlling, ask for guidance about the steps you can take to address the imbalance.

- Look for positive and practical strategies that can be implemented in your daily life.

- Consider the resources available, who can help you, when you will implement the ideas and the possible outcomes.

- Notice how you feel when you have made your plans. If you have any doubts, seek professional assistance so that support is available to you before any decisions are implemented.

LESSON 5

WHEN LOVE IS A SHIPWRECK, ALWAYS REBUILD ON DRY GROUND

Inspiration from Spirit:

Those who insist you join them are usually afraid to travel alone. You become tied to the consequences of their decisions, and such actions may hinder your progress. Ask yourself this: "What is it you seek to be joined to and whom does it serve?
Choose wisely, for your shared vibration attracts the future that awaits you."

I am an appalling sailor and easily get seasick.

Despite this, Merv and Maggie are two of my closest friends. They live on a catamaran, and if a full risk assessment has been conducted and there is a helicopter on emergency standby for my evacuation, I am sometimes invited to spend time on their boat.

WHEN LOVE IS A SHIPWRECK, ALWAYS REBUILD ON DRY GROUND

On one of these sojourns, a wind sprang up entirely without my permission. Although we were safely tucked away in a creek, a long journey back to the mainland was necessary the next morning. I eyed the white-capped waves dancing just beyond the creek's mouth uneasily.

Merv took a swig of his beer and seemed genuinely concerned as he asked, *"You know the only sure cure for sea-sickness, don't you?"*

I must admit, my hopes lifted. My partner was currently building a large boat and his dearest wish was to cruise the coastal waters *with me*. I never saw that coming when I let a sunflower change my destiny.

I was ready for a miracle.

"No," I replied with interest. *"What's the sure cure for seasickness?"*

"Sitting under a palm tree," answered Merv wryly.

Actually, I knew his humor was tenuous. Looking at that ocean, he already wished I was there.

The point to this seemingly flippant anecdote is that the only safe place to assess a relationship shipwreck is on the beach. It is impossible to let go of the pain while you are on the ocean's floor, clinging to your love-boat.

At some point you must look up and swim hard for the light.

Taking time out of a relationship gives us the emotional and physical space to look for landmarks in our commitment to our partner. Tuning into our hearts, we can feel whether the relationship is salvageable. If it is, we need to know the costs and whether it is wise to pay.

A decision to pay in effort and promises is not the hard part. The hard part is being able to give these things freely without resentment. This is where wisdom enters the process.

Acts of service are wonderful, but if you play the role of the martyr, history suggests you will probably get burned. You owe it to everyone in the relationship to make choices that will enrich rather than diminish you.

> *Ultimately, no matter how others feel, you can take responsibility for only yourself. This life was given to you and the gift of choice is yours. It does not belong to someone who wants to control, manipulate, or guilt you into loving them.*

Remember that when you are home in the spirit world, it is *your* decisions that will be examined in your life's review. You have to optimize your soul's opportunities to learn, without harming others. That is why you are here.

Choosing for our highest aspect of self is never selfish. The smaller self is the ego-driven persona we do battle with every time a new whim has to be satisfied. Many of our motives are propelled by this smaller self; however, to be spiritually aware of the purpose behind our relationships, we need to talk to the other one. We need to contact the author of our play.

Communicating with your High Self requires you to sit under that palm tree in quiet contemplation and feel into your motives for wanting to leave or stay. You need to determine whether these motives are grounded in positive, expansive energy or if they make you feel uneasy and constricted.

If you are being manipulated by a partner who wants control, you will feel unsettled and perhaps even anxious when you tune into your relationship's vibration.

Do not ignore any shifts in feelings that signal you to have caution. This is an important opportunity to examine whether the relationship you are assessing is worth salvaging. Ignoring subtle messages at this time invites future pain.

Choosing for the High Self

Choosing the High Self means one person might stay in a relationship while another person having the same kind of relationship might leave. Both actions can be appropriate. If service to others is their Soul's lesson, then one partner may feel that staying is the right path. Another partner, whose lesson is to develop independence, may leave because they need freedom to grow.

Kerri-Anne's Story

Ten years ago, a friend of mine passed into the spirit world. Kerri-Anne and I had been like sisters since we were four years old, so when she died suddenly in her sleep at the age of fifty-one, it was a tremendous shock. Throughout her life she was vivacious, flirtatious and oozed energy. She enjoyed champagne, parties and travel.

One night, after visiting her mother and sister, she went to sleep and never woke up.

Suddenly, her life made sense to me. At a soul level, she had known she had fewer days than most to enjoy whatever love she could embrace, and she had taken her opportunities as they came. I am grateful her spirit shone through convention and allowed her to do so. She was my teacher, showing me it is okay to lighten up, be carefree and have fun.

A fulfilling life does not have to be earned; it just needs to be chosen.

Judgment

When we understand that each person's lessons are unique, judgment flies out of the window. It has to; every space inside us denies it a home.

Judgment is rejected because we know we are never truly abandoned or alone. When we realize that those who have hurt us may be members of our soul family, compassion arises spontaneously. If their choices enhance their soul's growth, then we need not interpret their actions as punishment or betrayal. Our contract with them may be complete, despite the human pain of loss.

Likewise, even unwise choices do not make them 'bad' or 'unlovable'. We are all spiritual beings and every person is loved.

Activity

This activity will allow you to consider the costs and benefits of continuing a relationship.

It is impossible to reach a balanced decision about whether a relationship is viable without considering the costs and benefits.

One way to see the situation more clearly is through a meditation that connects with your High Self. Connecting with your High Self means you take responsibility for your decision-making, which is important.

When you connect with your High Self, you gain access to perspectives not frequently available. You may receive insights about your soul contract and whether salvaging or leaving a relationship is the best choice for your soul's growth.

Meditation – Perspectives From Your High Self

Step 1	Sit or lie in a comfortable position. Focus your attention on your breath and feel yourself relaxing. Visualize your heart center opening as your inner light expands and shines brightly.
	Connect with the brilliant White Light of the Source (God, Divine Spirit or whatever name you prefer). Feel the Light entering the crown of your head, pouring through you and out the soles of your feet.
Step 2	See or imagine this White Light flooding your entire environment. Say to yourself, *"The Light protects me. The Light surrounds me. I am Light."*
	Let your inner light and the Light from the Source merge to become one. Allow yourself to relax.
Step 3	Scan your body, gently releasing each muscle in turn. Breathe the White Light down into your abdomen and relax deeper as you exhale.
	Let your imagination help you with the next part of the journey.

Step 4	Imagine that you are being drawn gently upwards, as if you are floating up through the crown of your head. Stay within the White Light. You feel as if a gentle magnet is drawing you higher and higher. It takes no effort on your part. Ask that you are lifted to the vibration required to meet with your High Self. Remain focused on your intention as you continue to drift higher into the Light. The further into the Light you travel, the higher your spiritual vibration becomes. Go gently and slowly; do not push or rush. Allow yourself to drift until you come to a natural halt. Relax here for a few minutes and bathe in the Light.
Step 5	Ask now that the wisdom of your High Self connects with your mind. It helps to imagine a bright light, which is your High Self's vibration, merging with your own. Feel, sense, or imagine the two lights joining as one. Rest for a minute or two to allow this process to occur and then ask questions about your relationship.

Step 6	Ask your High Self to reveal the costs involved for all relevant persons if you stay. Next, ask to understand the benefits, if any, of continuing the relationship. Take this opportunity to look at the motives of each person, and the likely outcomes of staying and leaving. Spend time listening to the answers without evaluating them. When you have finished, thank your High Self. Know you can always access this wisdom when you calm and lift your vibration.
Step 7	Sense or visualize yourself coming down through the White Light, floating back into your body. Feel energy flowing out through the soles of your feet and into the Earth to make sure you have completely reconnected to your physical life.

If you wish, record the insights you gained in your journal. Reflect on the information received. Make wise choices that consider the costs and benefits of potential decisions about your relationship's future.

LESSON 6
IGNORE THE DOOMSAYERS. AUDIT YOUR FRIENDS' ADVICE

Inspiration from Spirit:

You are the instrument. Let the breath of your inner voice play your notes.

Friends vs Lovers Loyalty Test

How friends love to predict the end of the world for those who don't follow their advice!

The friends I am referring to here include everyone who assumes it is their duty to make sure we choose the outcome they think is best for us. They could be family members, colleagues, friends and all who believe they have a stake in our relationships.

We need to be aware of their agenda, because they will exact a high price if they do not achieve their preferred result.

If you have not yet experienced the friend who declares *they* can't go through another relationship trauma with you, then remain vigilant, because most likely you will. In every crisis there are friends who threaten to jump ship unless you ditch a partner they never liked in the first place.

Once these friends come clean and express their true feelings, you are involuntarily drawn into a competition you never wanted to enter. Your decision about your partner is suddenly the measure of who you value most – the friend, who has stood faithfully by you, keeping their peace for the sake of your friendship, or your disgraced lover who, in your friend's eyes, has never been good enough for you in the first place.

This is a very uncomfortable position to be trapped in. You find yourself wondering how friendship and your partnership suddenly sit on opposing ends of a seesaw, where someone has to win, and someone has to lose. Suddenly, you cannot have both any longer and it makes no sense, because up until now, it appeared you could. The world feels foreign and insecure when these shifts in loyalties occur. It is like sensing the tectonic plates sliding beneath you without being able to prevent the earthquake.

Why does it happen?

What causes the seemingly strong foundations of friendship to crumble in a relationship crisis?

The answer is complex.

- While true friends never want you to stay in a damaging relationship, beware of others who covertly desire that your relationship ends. The tricky part is that the motives of this second group are often unconscious, and hence hidden even from themselves. Any challenge you make will bring accusations you don't understand or appreciate them, so be aware that these friends bring a minefield of explosions as punishment for unheeded advice.

- It maybe they feel protective of you and mistakenly believe they must shield you from the choices that are yours to make.

- Perhaps they are projecting their own fears of being unable to cope in a similar situation, sending you emotional ultimatums instead of recognizing their true feelings.

- It may even be that they are envious or jealous of you, and at an unconscious level do not feel that you deserve happiness. This is especially common if their life's decisions have been limiting and unforgiving. They demand the same from you, since your willingness to forgive and heal highlights the possibility that their choices have not created a loving and happy life.

IGNORE THE DOOMSAYERS. AUDIT YOUR FRIENDS' ADVICE

I had my share of 'doomsayers' when my partner and I decided to recommit to our relationship. One friend wanted to send me to the other side of the world, just to spare me from my own bad decision making.

Others were genuinely dismayed with my decision and struggled with what this meant for my friendship with them. Although they wanted to protect me, the *friend versus partner loyalty-test* tugged fiercely at my heartstrings and sponsored an unhealthy relationship with guilt.

"Whose life is it?" I wondered at times, and yet that question was unfair to them.

Watching someone you love get hurt on an ongoing basis is not something any of us would choose to do. My pain was hurting them, opening old wounds that hadn't healed.

> *We need to remember that every person has met pain somewhere on their journey, and our decisions can trigger unhappy memories from their pasts.*

My friends had the right to step back until they felt comfortable about how my relationship with my partner would work out.

After all, they didn't have all the facts. My life was not theirs to live. I, alone, had to be responsible for my decisions.

Two of my closest friends kept faith in my partner. Their trust in my intelligence to know what was right for me and their willingness to see the best in him gave me the conviction to create the future I wanted.

Be gentle with your friends and try to understand the motives behind their behavior. However, mostly, be gentle with yourself. Do not let blackmail, guilt or other people's unconscious fears form the basis of your decision making. Ignore the doomsayers and audit your friends' advice.

If you are ready to move forward, with or without your relationship intact, now is the time to do so. Take the step, and do not look backwards again.

There's only one place you will find the next moment of your life, and it is never where you have been. To create a different future, you need to let go of the past.

Activity

This activity will help you discern your inner voice and lovingly deal with your friends' advice.

> When facing powerful expectations from others, you need to return to your center and find your inner voice.
>
> Within you is a calm, wise presence that is not swayed by the demanding winds that try to blow it from one direction to another. You will hear it as your own voice or thought.

1. Tune into that voice. Your inner voice will not be emotionally needy, or even too passionately attached to a particular outcome. It will be firm, reassuring and steady.

2. Consider, when friends demand a particular outcome, learn to discern the difference between their voice and your own. Lovingly see their fears, motives or genuine concerns according to the intentions behind their words.

    a. Do they wish the best for you? If so, thank them, but explain you must follow your own feelings.

    b. If they are unconsciously trying to undermine you, thank them anyway, but create space between them and you, so they cannot damage your resolve.

The important thing to know is that your own wise voice comes from stillness and acceptance, not from passion, jealousy or need.

When you can feel and sense *that* inner voice, you can believe that whatever outcome evolves, you have the strength to endure the journey.

Meditation - Inner Voices

Step 1	Find a quiet place where you will be undisturbed. Settle down, relax, and fill yourself with the Light of the Source. Listen to the range of voices, messages and concerns that have been offered to you by others. Hear them all. Disrespect none. Feel into the motives and concerns behind this advice. Notice the tone and the intention of each person's counsel.
Step 2	Be sure you have weighed up every point of view offered. Then, turn down the volume on the sea of voices that crave your attention, and listen to the voice within.
Step 3	Once again, you are connecting with your High Self. In the stillness of your own inner knowing, how does your inner voice respond to your friends' advice? What does your inner voice need to communicate to you? Give yourself time to hear what is said and felt. Perhaps, once again, you will write all that is received for reflection at a later time.

LESSON 7
LEAVE THE PAST IN THE PAST

Inspiration from Spirit:

Living in the past is like trying to breathe in a room that is low in oxygen. Close the door to this room and open yourself to the potential that awaits you. The purpose of the present is to create, for we are all creators. Be in the present; create in the fullness of all you are.

While you are resting under your palm tree, pondering whether to flee from your relationship or launch a salvage mission, consider another important question.

Can you leave the hurts of the past in the past?

I won't pretend dismissing the past is easy, but the past is an anchor. It will weigh you down and burden you forever if you let it.

I struggled with releasing the past during the sad times when my partner and I were in and out of our relationship. I rehashed old events, wanting certainty, clarity and commitment. All this achieved was further destabilization and confusion. I wanted a definite destination for something that could be only a journey of exploration.

On the morning that I found the courage to commit one last time, I promised myself I would never bring up the hurts of the past again. Years later, I am still true to my intention.

Moving away from the history of a painful relationship is one of the scariest steps I have taken. However, I knew that if we were to have a chance of success, I had to melt my resentments and learn to trust again. That's hard when so many decisions in the present are based on impacts from the past.

When you decide to work on important emotional issues, it can feel like walking out onto a rickety bridge with a deep ravine below. I know I felt that way.

My success did not occur by chance. While I pledged not to dissect the past with my partner, I did seek counseling and explored my fears with professional help. I reached a stage where I knew that no matter what happened, I would survive without damaging my integrity or sanity. I learned not to be hyper-vigilant, realizing that every quiet mood was not a sign of doom. It took enormous resolve to let the past stay in the past, but I did it and if you choose, so can you.

Whether you are leaving a relationship, considering a new one or hoping to rebuild, you need to climb down from the carousel that will keep you stuck in a ring of blame forever, disconnect the power and walk away.

The past will rob you of the infinite potential for happiness in the present. Seek help. Let it go.

Activity

This exercise will assist you to leave unhelpful memories from the past behind you.

Preparation

You can prepare for this exercise by selecting events and memories that you wish to release. This may make the actual task easier once you begin.

Meditation – Leave The Past Behind

Step 1	Sit or lie in a comfortable position. Focus your attention on your breath and feel yourself relaxing. Visualize your heart center opening as your inner light expands and shines brightly.
Step 2	Connect with the brilliant White Light of the Source (God, Divine Spirit, or whatever name you prefer). Feel the Light entering the crown of your head, pouring through you and out the soles of your feet.

Step 3	See or imagine this White Light flooding your entire environment. Say to yourself, "*The Light protects me. The Light surrounds me. I am Light.*" Let your inner light and the Light from the Source merge to become one.
Step 4	Allow yourself to relax. Scan your body, gently releasing each muscle in turn. Breathe the White Light down into your abdomen and relax deeper as you exhale.
Step 5	Visualize yourself at the top of a long staircase. There are ten steps. At the bottom is a large steel door that is closed. Make your way down the staircase. As your foot touches every step, feel yourself relaxing further. Count the steps down in your mind from ten to one. Do not hurry; descend with the timing of each breath.

Part A - The Vault

Step 6	When you finally reach the bottom of the staircase, place your hand on the doorhandle and open the door. See that the door leads into a large vault, about the size of a room. In the centre of the vault is steel chest with its lid open. Next to the chest is a chair. Walk to the chair, sit down, and take 3 deep breaths.
Step 7	Place in this steel chest all the painful memories, hurts, regrets, anger, guilt, and shame you are holding within you. Ask your spiritual helpers to assist if you need their support. Reflect on each item, as you toss it into the open chest. Take as long as you need. If you cannot release something unhelpful to you, frame an affirmation that destroys the energy. Then place it in the chest. **For example**: *"I forgive myself for the pain I caused my husband and free myself from guilt. I accept my lessons and move on."*

Step 8	When you are satisfied that everything necessary is in the chest, close the lid. There are seven padlocks on the lid, each with a key. As you lock each padlock affirm: *"I seal my past with love and forgiveness."* You have the only keys, should you ever need to add more memories to your chest.

Part B - Cord Cutting

Step 9	Bring to mind all the people you wish to release from your life as though they are standing in front of you. In a moment, you will find a pair of glasses in your hands that link you to your clairvoyant gifts. When you wear these glasses, you will be able to see the cords of energy between you and those who have kept you tied to the past, hurt, or limited you in any way. These cords will appear in the form of energy lines, and may resemble cobwebs, ropes, or energetic chains. Allow your imagination to guide you. The glasses are in your hands now. Put the glasses on.

Step 10	As you face each person, see or sense where the cords exit you and where the cords connect to them. Are you joined between your hearts? Emotional centers (abdomen)? Minds? Sexual centers? Allow yourself to know. Working with one person at a time, cut the cords that are no longer healthy or helpful to you. You can use a sword, call on Archangel Michael or destroy the cords with any method you choose. You have the power. The moment the cords are disconnected, they begin withering away. Dispose of the old cords in a way that is comfortable to you. You might consider consumption by fire, burial in the earth, dispersal in the air or transformation in the Light.
Step 11	Leave the vault and close the door. Make your way back up the stairs, counting from one to ten. With each step you become a little more aware of your surroundings. When you reach the top of the stairs, you are fully awake. Take a deep breath and open your eyes.

LEAVE THE PAST IN THE PAST

In the coming days, remind yourself that the issues and memories in the chest are locked away.

Remember that you are free from unhelpful patterns and ties to old relationships. Reinforce your new freedom and feel the changes right down to the cells in your body.

LESSON 8

WEEDS ARE JUST OVERACHIEVERS. LEARN TO LOVE THEM.

Inspiration from Spirit:

Be gentle with yourself. We will not give up on you; therefore, do not give up on yourself. When you feel peaceful, you are closest to your true nature and to Divinity. Do not be afraid or weary, for the Soul's journey is timeless. You cannot measure growth in human years nor should you fear the time taken for evolution. We see you as beautiful beings whose lights already shine. Protect your heart. Protect your song-lines. They are the essence of who you are. All is well. We repeat. All is well.

I am not ashamed to admit that I feel empathy with almost all things. I talk to trees, dogs, flowers and people I pass on the street. I believe everything feels my respect at some level.

WEEDS ARE JUST OVERACHIEVERS. LEARN TO LOVE THEM

I also tolerate insects. Spiders and cockroaches are just being what they are according to their evolutions' blueprints. I cannot blame them for that. They belong as equally to the Divine creation as does a beautiful rose. The fact my human nature appreciates a rose and is inclined to recoil from a cockroach does not make the cockroach any less worthy than the rose in the creative design of the Universe.

This is something my partner and I disagree on. No shopping list is complete until he has checked his supplies of insect spray. If a long spray of poison doesn't kill the unwelcome house guests, I'm pretty sure drowning will.

I also have a soft spot for weeds, mainly because they are so much like us. That statement is a compliment.

Weeds do not receive the accolades given to carnations, azaleas, tulips and other gorgeous flowers. Few homes display weeds' achievements in a vase. However, they try hard to make the best of what they are, and they do what every plant comes into life to do - to grow and reproduce. They cling to barren rocky outcrops and bloom with all their might, throwing their little hearts into their one chance of expression. Weeds are just as true to their Divinity as is the perfect rose.

When you take the time to look at the tiny flowers on weeds, you cannot help but admire their beauty. They may be small and pugnacious but face it - weeds are just overachievers. They are merely doing what they were put on Earth to do. As my Sunday school teacher told me long ago, *"There is a place for everything in God's garden."*

It came to me in a revelation that a heart that is open to love, can also love a weed.

I am not suggesting weeds should invade your garden. I just mean that beauty can come in tough little parcels, and if we cannot recognize beauty when it looks us in the face, how can we hope to see it in ourselves or in others?

In reality, most of us are like little flowers, working hard, often without the acknowledgement or love we deserve. We are beautiful at our core, fragile and hardy at the same time, giving life the best contribution we can. We need to love ourselves for that.

When you reflect on your current circumstances, you will realize that a string of decisions, beliefs and emotions have brought you to where you now are. Each of the actions associated with those decisions, beliefs and emotions has polished you like the diamond that you are. The stone may still have rough spots here and there, but the glint of strength and beauty always shines.

Sometimes you have struggled to get out of bed in the morning, but you did it. Sometimes you have faced heart-breaking loss, but you kept fighting for what you believed was fair or right. Often you were protecting others. Sometimes, I hope, you were protecting yourself.

Acknowledge the journey you are taking. Love yourself for the courage and compassion you have already shown. Stay strong for yourself and those you care about. Be tenacious and live fully; like those tiny weeds, never give up.

Divinity does not require us to be a great leader, a saint, or a sporting legend in order to fulfil our destinies. For millions of people, finding their next meal or clean drink of water is demanding enough. Our Soul's growth is not about living grand lives.

Whether we are struggling to feed our families or earning a million dollars a year, what counts is our minute by minute choices and how they impact us and those around us. Are we resonating with integrity and truth? Are we consciously choosing our actions and words to make a positive difference in the world, or are we automatic robots whose lives pass by in a dream?

Karma is an evolving process.

Everything has brought us to the present moment. Our Soul's growth reflects the sum of all decisions since our inception.

Our responsibility is simple - to be the best we can be in all circumstances.

In recognizing the small acts of kindness that surround us, we open ourselves to love. A touch of a hand, a smile, a compliment, a wish for good health - these are gestures of the heart that we too often miss, yet we can consciously elect to fill our lives with loving kindness.

Every thought and deed can be a channel for love if we choose to make it so.

When we appreciate beauty everywhere, regardless of the packaging, our hearts open. Weeds, insects, roses seem equally Divine. This is when love yearns to manifest.

Activity

This exercise will help you appreciate the qualities in yourself.

- Imagine that you are your best friend or someone who loves you.

- Write a letter from their perspective that expresses appreciation for the positive qualities you possess, large and small. Name those qualities, and explain how and when they manifest.

- If this feels hard, remember that beauty comes in resilient little parcels, and there is much resilience within you.

- Have courage and be gentle with yourself. Write.

THE ASPECTS OF LOVE

Inspiration from Spirit:

Every instant is an opportunity to create love. Search for the gap, which will you feel as ripples in the life-force between you and each person you meet. In this gap of recognition, reach for that Soul and do your work.

In the meditation group I facilitate, we have a different discussion topic each week. On one occasion the topic was, 'What is love?'

The variety of responses was almost as numerous as respondents. Some thought love was a feeling, others felt love was an emotion that could not be defined, and one friend declared love was neither a feeling nor an emotion because *love just is*.

"Fair enough," I thought, "But *love just is what?*" The teacher in me struggled with such an enigmatic definition, yet the philosopher in me loved it. I am comfortable with God's assertion in the Old Testament of the Holy Bible, "*I am that I am.*" It makes sense that the Divine is beyond my understanding, so I am content with not knowing the details.

Given that, I should be equally comfortable with the definition,
Love is what it is.

Yet, I am not. We use the word in such a casual way that love's definition is loose at best.

Lust, obsession, and romantic idealism are only three of many guises that mask themselves as love. Some of these impostors are dangerous, blaming love for the need to control others.

The courts are filled with domestic violence perpetrators who claim 'love' drove them to harm their partner or family. On the opposite side of the scales sit those who are so unable to take personal responsibility that they cling to the lives of their partners, claiming 'love' makes them spend every moment together. There seems little personal growth in that.

The qualities of love

It took me more than forty years to realize that love, in the purest sense, is wrapped up in a bundle of qualities, each of which is an aspect of the whole. These qualities include

- ♥ Gratitude
- ♥ Honor
- ♥ Compassion
- ♥ Forgiveness and
- ♥ Truth

As a heart opens to offer these qualities to life, so love pours back into this heart. There is no emptying through effort, only refilling in a continuous flow. As you give of yourself with pure intention, so the Universe responds to you.

LESSON 9

GRATITUDE IS THE FIRST ASPECT OF LOVE

Inspiration from Spirit:

Gratitude is like an opening flower. Each petal that unfolds to the sunlight reveals more of the beauty within. When your heart expresses appreciation for life, your inner light radiantly shines.

Gratitude arises from an open heart

Gratitude is an aspect of love because it is arises from an open heart. Regardless of the challenges we face or the deprivations we have experienced, life offers us opportunities to be thankful.

The beauty of nature - its healing colors and vibrations - is worthy of daily gratitude. Consider the millions of expressions of blue and green across our planet in oceans, waterways, sky, trees and plants. Remember the hues of a gorgeous sunset and know that healing vibrations of gold and pink lift and soothe our energy. Truly, nature is a gift that we can appreciate in many daily moments.

Gratitude comes without thought because it comes from the heart. A smile from a stranger when we are having a hard day or an act of kindness from a friend sparks instant gratitude. A person may feel they have nothing to give, but kindness is always a treasured gift for one who needs it.

Opportunities to offer gratitude are many. Our eyes, ears and hearts just need to be awake to our blessings.

Gratitude heals us

When we give thanks, with no expectation of receiving in return, we forget our own problems and allow our High Self to rise. Gratitude is healing to our spirit.

It is helpful to remember that love is expressed in different ways, and while a partner may not do or say what you desire, perhaps in other ways they demonstrate their affection. Your preferred means of receiving love, may not match their capacity to offer it.

A practical person may demonstrate love through helpful deeds such as mowing lawns, cooking meals, caring for the home, managing finances and so on. Words of love may be difficult, and this person may not see any point in sentimental gifts or occasions.

A person who values words or tokens of love, often finds it difficult to understand and appreciate a practical partner, and the reverse is also true. A practical person may feel their affection is obvious; just look at everything they are doing to keep things running smoothly. Why should more be needed? Why should they make a fuss of Valentine's Day or even an anniversary? You should know how they feel about you, right?

If only this were true. Many partners misunderstand their partner's feelings, because love is not offered in the way they want or need to receive it.

Activity

This exercise guides you to acknowledge positive qualities within your partner. Set your intention to be honest and non-judgmental.

---

1. **Make a list of the most important ways in which you need love to be expressed to you.**

   Here are some possibilities to get you started.

   - ♥ Words - being told you are loved, reassurance, encouragement, praise, compliments
   - ♥ Physical intimacy - sex, holding hands, cuddling, touching
   - ♥ Emotional intimacy - sharing feelings, listening to you, making time to be together

- ♥ Gifts and tokens of affection - gifts on anniversaries and birthdays, cards on Valentine's Day, jewellery, flowers

- ♥ Loyalty - faithfulness, honesty, standing up for you, standing by you, being your best friend, respecting your family, believing in you

- ♥ Practical acts - helping with tasks, looking after you, maintaining a comfortable home, providing financial security

Please add other options as they come to your mind.

2. **Now write a second list that records the ways your partner shows their affection for you. Consider ways which are not on your list, but still demonstrate your partner's attempts at affection.**

- ♥ Be open-minded and fair. Not receiving what you prefer may not be a reliable indicator of whether your partner loves you.

- ♥ Assuming there are some positive items on your partner's list, take time to feel gratitude for these expressions of affection or love. Better still, express your gratitude to your partner directly.

3. Discussing your findings and inviting your partner to complete the same activity can be helpful in opening new understanding and communication between you.

♥ If there are items on your list that are non-negotiable, and your partner admits they cannot or will not offer love to you in this way, then you have additional information for your decision-making about your future.

LESSON 10

HONOR IS THE SECOND ASPECT OF LOVE

Inspiration from Spirit:

Find your integrity and do not sway from its substance. Integrity's expression may be different in every person you meet but respect must be offered regardless. You cannot judge another's life-path and you do not know the Soul's lessons imprinted before their birth.

The essence of honoring another person is respecting them, whether they are similar to us or different, whether they conform to our preferences, or not.

When we honor ourselves, we connect to our Divinity. When we connect to our Divinity, we automatically respect others.

> *The memory that we are all souls in physical form frees us from prejudice and hatred. We sense in every person a light that shines just like our own.*

We are able to honour them as spiritual beings because we respect their journey.

Conflict at an energetic level is healed when we recognize another person's Divinity. By offering respect to that person's High Self, petty human squabbles dissipate. Try this for yourself; it works.

At the quantum level, everything is energy, and the energetic impacts of our thoughts, emotions and actions ripple throughout the Universe. We need to take responsibility for our life and the impacts of our influence on the lives of others.

Activity

Preparation for this meditation

Consider a person with whom you would like to build a more positive relationship. This activity is particularly helpful in softening relationships with someone with whom you are experiencing conflict or difficult communication.

Meditation - Honor The High Self

Step 1	Connect with the brilliant White Light of the Source (God, Divine Spirit or whatever name you prefer). Feel the Light entering the crown of your head, pouring through you and out the soles of your feet. See or imagine this White Light flooding your entire environment. Say to yourself, "*The Light protects me. The Light surrounds me. I am Light.*" Let your inner light and the Light from the Source merge to become one.
Step 2	Sit or lie in a comfortable position. Focus your attention on your breath and feel yourself relaxing. Visualize your heart center opening as your inner light expands and shines brightly. Let your imagination help you with the next part of the journey.
Step 3	Imagine that you are being drawn gently upwards, as if you are floating up through the crown of your head. Stay within the White Light. You feel as if a gentle magnet is drawing you higher and higher. It takes no effort on your part.

Step 4	Ask that you are lifted to the vibration required to meet with your High Self. Remain focused on your intention as you continue to drift higher into the Light. The further into the Light you travel, the higher your spiritual vibration becomes. Go gently and slowly; do not push or rush. Allow yourself to drift until you come to a natural halt. Ask now that the wisdom of your High Self connects with your mind. It helps to imagine a bright light, which is your High Self's vibration, merging with your own. Feel, sense, or imagine the two lights joining as one.
Step 5	It is time to invite the High Self of your guest to join you for a meeting. See them as a bright light that draws close to you, and know that despite any current conflicts, they also seek harmony. This is your opportunity to speak together in order to resolve conflict or create a closer understanding of each other's viewpoints. Welcome them by affirming, *"The Divinity in me respects the Divinity in you."* Then begin your communication and observe the response.

Step 6	Place yourself in the other person's position. Feel their intentions and their needs in this situation. Be a listener, not just the communicator. Be prepared to learn new perspectives about the issue or relationship. It is possible you are unaware of key information that would change or soften your viewpoint. It is not necessary to hear words. Feel the mutual sharing of energy flowing between you. It will be unconsciously understood.
Step 7	When the meeting has finished, thank your guest, allow yourself to drift down through the Light, and feel yourself fully present in your physical body. Move your fingers and toes, stretch, and open your eyes.

LESSON 11

COMPASSION IS THE THIRD ASPECT OF LOVE

Inspiration from Spirit:

Compassion is Soul-food. Give it freely, for it flows from a spring that never runs dry.

Compassion comes from a genuine desire to ease another's suffering. Healing energy streams from our hearts when we are filled with a compassionate intention.

Compassion recognises we are spiritual brothers and sisters in the same human family. It differs from sympathy because compassion does not evoke pity. Like gratitude, compassion is a softening energy, opening our hearts to love.

In offering compassion, we receive compassion ourselves and have the wisdom to know we deserve it. We soften our attitude to ourselves and see our life's experiences

COMPASSION IS THE THIRD ASPECT OF LOVE

through our heart-mind. The heart-mind blends love and reason, allowing us to feel and see relationships without judgment. The heart-mind unites knowledge and compassion, providing a loving basis for our feelings and decisions.

During meditation, we have the opportunity to send compassion to all life on the planet. Since energy follows thought, our prayerful meditation carries compassion to countries in turmoil, poverty and despair.

Compassion benefits the land, the sea, the rivers, the air; every aspect of Creation possesses consciousness and is sensitive to healing energy. Earth is our spiritual mother and our sincere desire for her healing helps restore harmony.

Compassion, with its inherent understanding, paves the way for a very special gift.

You have already sensed it in other forms, and it is time now to accept it yourself.

Activity

Meditation - Compassion for the World

Step 1	Make yourself comfortable, either sitting or lying down. Take the time to let your body find its most relaxed position and close your eyes.
	Allow any thoughts that come into your mind to float away as though you are watching leaves falling from a tree. You may notice them, but they need not concern you. Just observe them and let them go.
	Connect now to the light in your heart and allow it to expand so that you are filled with light.
Step 2	Imagine, sense, or feel yourself under a shower of White Light that comes from the Source. See this Light filling your aura, tumbling around you so that your energy-field is bright and shining.
	Feel this Light entering the crown of your head and filling your body. Allow this energy to run down your legs, into your feet, and deep into the earth, anchoring and grounding your energies. See and feel yourself part of an infinite energy-field that links earth and sky.

COMPASSION IS THE THIRD ASPECT OF LOVE

Step 3 | Sense the colors that resonate to the energy of compassion. The colors you choose will be individual to you. Focus on feeling compassion and imagine your colors flowing out from your heart until you are filled with their energy.

Know that no matter what you have done, or who you have hurt, you are worthy of compassion.

You are a loving spiritual being who is a spark of the Divine Spirit. Stay in that energy for as long as you need.

Step 4

Now visualize Earth as a green and blue planet, spinning in front of you in space.

Send the compassion that is flowing out of your heart to Earth and imagine Earth completely infused and surrounded with this loving energy.

Let compassion reach those areas that have strife, poverty and pollution. Allow your compassion to bring healing to the air, water, vegetation and soil

Send compassion to the animal kingdom and humans throughout the world.

As you are connecting with all life forms, affirm:

"Divine Spirit (or your term for the Higher Power), *make me an instrument of your compassion."*

Repeat this affirmation as you send loving, healing, compassion from your heart to the entire planet, the Universe and into the spiritual worlds.

Know your capacity to give is infinite because you are linked to the energy of the Divine Spirit - the energy of the White Light.

Step 5	When you feel it is time to return to the present moment, see your energy-field filled with light and seal it in a golden bubble.
	Take several deep breaths as you bring yourself back to full waking consciousness. Take your time. Ground yourself with a glass of water and enjoy the rest of your day or evening.

LESSON 12
FORGIVENESS IS THE FOURTH ASPECT OF LOVE

Inspiration from Spirit:

Tread gently, for you cannot judge when a lesson is done or when a flower is ready to be plucked. You are a traveller who may choose your path, but do not trample or disrespect another. You are all children of Light and all are loved.

It may seem strange that forgiveness occurs so late in a book about love, yet since no-one can be taught to forgive, this lesson is in the perfect position.

The secret to forgiveness is realizing we have nothing real remaining that requires it.

I say nothing *real*, because the phantoms of hurt and rage may still throw their shadows on the backdrop of your play. They may still attempt to draw you into their dramas, to rouse you into judgment, but you know now that they are tricksters without form, puppets without a puppeteer.

During your journey back into yourself, forgiveness has accompanied your every step.

- It was present when you remembered your soul family, allowing you to feel compassion for those who have hurt you.
- It was there when you made peace with the toad, prompting you to honor your own hurt and shame.
- Forgiveness gave you the courage to accept responsibility for your life, and through gratitude's eyes, forgiveness helped you love a tiny weed.

Does it get any better than that? What greater contribution to the Universe can you now make because you are able to love in the largest sense of the word, free from the bondage of judgment? Let the possibilities take root deep inside you as you sense your future expanding.

There is one last lesson to learn and it requires a warrior's heart. Don't be afraid; you are ready. It is time to stand up for your truth.

Activity

This exercise will help you to clarify your relationship with your partner. Ideally, it includes their involvement as well as your own.

The list of non-negotiables

At this point in your journey, you will know what you need - the non-negotiables - for you to be happy. This activity requires you to briefly put your current relationship to one side and focus on what you most need from *any* partner so that you feel loved and content.

> 1. **Create a list of only those qualities that you *must* have; it should not be longer than necessary nor include anything you consider of minor importance.**
>
> It is not about telling the other person what they have to do for you or how they need to change. Rather, it is about you owning your power and expressing what you need in a successful relationship with any partner. Take responsibility for what you need.
>
> **Begin your list with a statement such as:**
>
> - *In order to feel content in a relationship, I need a partner who.....*
>
> - Here are some of my 'non-negotiables' in a relationship.

In order to feel content in a relationship, I need a partner who:

- Is always faithful to me
- Encourages me to keep learning and growing
- Trusts me
- Loves me for who I am
- Is gentle, kind, and respectful
- Wants to be intimate with me
- Sees us growing older together

Your list may be more specific according to current circumstances.

2. **Next, write specific behaviors and attitudes that allow you to know when you are receiving the items on your list.**

- For example, *faithfulness*, might mean that your partner is never involved sexually or romantically with anyone else.
- Being *encouraged* might mean that your partner supports you in further study or in following your passions.

The aim is to share with your partner what your 'non-negotiables' look like in action.

3. Invite your partner to complete the same activity. Again, this is not where they tell you how they want you to change or behave differently. Their list must match the style in which you wrote yours and provide specific examples.

- Do this in private and only share your lists when each of you is finished. At an appropriate time, when you are not stressed, under the influence of alcohol or likely to be interrupted, share the lists. Do not fall into the temptation of interrupting, blaming each other or discussing the past.

- If your partner is unwilling to participate or thinks it is a waste of time, that in itself provides you with information.

- This activity helps clarify whether a partnership has run it course or has positive potential in the future. It is a basis for honest evaluation and negotiation.

LESSON 13

TRUTH IS THE FINAL ASPECT OF LOVE

Inspiration from Spirit:

If you do not have a center, then how can you stand?
If you do not have will, then whose wheel will drive you?
If attachments are the fullness of your spirit, then where is the room for growth?
You do not learn by withholding, but only by flowing.
Follow the flowing river of truth, and inevitably you will discover yourself.

Standing up for your truth requires the heart-quality of courage.

It may seem like madness to your family and friends that you have shed your anger, shame and guilt, leaving you truly happy and light. Some will want to pull you back into the 'play', urging you to forget the soul contracts and lessons you have discovered. They will want you to approve of their bad behaviour and continue unhelpful relationships. This is now your choice, not your destiny.

TRUTH IS THE FINAL ASPECT OF LOVE

Standing up for your truth is not about championing great causes; it is about quietly championing your own. It is about having the resilience to weather the disbelief of those who have not shared your journey. It is finding the courage to stand firmly in the place where your heart needs you to be.

When we speak our truth, our spirit responds. Our vibration resonates with our words. Wonderful growth comes simply from living our truth.

Mahatma Gandhi stated:

"If we could change ourselves, the tendencies in the world would also change. As a man changes his own nature, so does the attitude of the world change towards him. This is the Divine Mystery supreme."

His words are often summarized into the simple statement:

Be the change you wish to see in the world.

Every person who chooses to live an ethical life is honoring the vibration of their Soul. When your vibration rises, your spiritual guides and loved ones draw closer, supporting your courage and faith. You will notice their signs and symbols and know how to read them. You will recognize the signposts you planted before you were born, and your life will begin to make sense.

Standing up for your truth is the greatest gift you can give yourself. It is the purest expression of love, because gratitude, honor, compassion and forgiveness rest firmly at its base.

Moving forward from this point is not difficult or complex. You already know what to do.

> **Seek only love.**
>
> **In situations where you feel confused, ask yourself, *"What would love do now?"***

Let the answer you receive guide your response.

In your relationships with partners, friends, colleagues, family and everyone on the planet, search for the Divine Light in every being, and love them for whom they are trying to be.

It does not matter if they have reached their goals, or even if they are awake to their soul journey in this life. They have all the time they need in the great design of the Universe to work things out. Know that Divinity sits within them, as it sits within you. Their failure, like yours, is not a possibility.

> ***Seek love in all things and seek only love. Then love will surely find you.***

Activity

This activity helps you connect to the truth within you.

Reflect on the statement below and consider your answers to the questions that follow:

Be The Change You Wish to See in the World.

Questions:

What is it you stand for? What is the essence of your truth? What qualities have a place in your heart?	
What will you commit to that honors the soul journey you are choosing?	

When you have finished contemplating the questions, write an affirmation that encapsulates who you are and where you are heading in your life.

Breathe it into every cell of your body. Say it aloud and repeat it often. This is your truth.

Let it forge a fire of determination and strength within.

Your Affirmation

EPILOGUE

It was another humid, Summer's day as I began the task of writing this book. After capturing the significance of the sunflower in the first chapter, I was excited to share my progress with my husband. Yes, we did make it to the altar despite the rocky path we chose in getting there.

He listened patiently as I read him my story and then asked casually,

"Have you seen your sunflowers yet? The ones I planted for you?"

My husband is the master of understatement and knows exactly when to share information for maximum impact.

It goes without saying that I had no idea we had sunflowers.

"What sunflowers?" I demanded, railing against his barely concealed mirth. "Where are they?"

It transpired that the sunflowers were growing down the narrow side of the house, near a papaya tree. Because the soil had been improved there, he had planted three sunflowers some weeks prior, and miraculously, they were blooming.

The only sunflowers grown in the nine years of our partnership coincided with my writing about sunflowers in this book.

EPILOGUE

However, synchronicity had not finished with me yet. About a week later I created the chapter on learning to love weeds. Once again, I was keen to share my efforts.
It was in the heat of the day when I went looking for my husband. He was neither in his office, nor in any room of the house, so I took my search outside. I figured he was passionate enough about building his ark that I would find him in the boat-shed. Strangely, he was not there, so I called John's name.

Finally, his voice came from the far end of the yard and I found him on his knees, working along the fence line.

Weeding.

I was speechless at the Universe's sense of humour.

To my horror, a row of little purple flowers, some might call them weeds, lay uprooted, and wilting in the sun.

Naturally, I rescued the flowers, hurried inside, and arranged them in a vase where they bloomed gratefully for a fortnight.

I am not confident my husband ever understood the amazement I felt about his weeding that day, but I know my spiritual friends are still laughing.

When you approach life with an open heart, believe me, the Universe knows how to send you weeds.

The best part is, you will love them.

LOVE ON THE OTHER SIDE

Personal Responses To Frequently Asked Questions

What is a soul family?

A soul family or soul group is comprised of a number of spirits who choose to work and grow together both on Earth and between lives.

While many of the group members may be at a similar level of development, there will also be one or more spirits with a greater level of experience who play guiding roles in the lives on Earth.

Some soul families are quite static and do not change, while others are dynamic and fluid. This is largely the choice of the individual members of the family; however, each spirit has a responsibility to continue to grow. A spirit who is progressing more quickly than others may spend time with other groups to continue their development.

Gender is not fixed in soul groups and so each spirit will experience lives in which they are male and female. Changing genders allows for a wider variety of lessons to be learned. In a range of human lives, the same spirit may play the role of your father, son, mother, daughter, friend and so on. This is why it is not helpful to despair too deeply over events that occur in one relationship in one lifetime.

You can usually tell who a member of your soul group is, by the connection you feel when your eyes make contact. The eyes are the windows to the soul.

If you meet a partner, family member or friend and feel like you have known them forever, there is a strong chance you have.

What is a soulmate?

The term soulmate refers to two spirits who are devoted to each other. It is true that some spirits frequently choose to incarnate as lovers and spouses. This is because they have a deep and loving bond which exists between them no matter where they are.

However, soulmates do not always come back to Earth as romantic partners. If being in a romantic relationship does not advance each Soul's growth, soulmates might choose to be family members, friends, colleagues and so on.

A soulmate might even make their partner's life difficult, to advance their partner's learning.

The concept of a soulmate is a human one, since in the spirit world gender is unimportant. This does not mean two spirits cannot feel deep love for each other. It is possible for spirits who have been a husband and wife or devoted lovers on Earth to remain as spouses until they are ready to resume their true genderless light-bodies.

They will be able to manipulate energy through thought to create a home and the environment they are familiar with while they become re-accustomed to the spirit world. If one partner has crossed first, this familiar setting will help the second partner to adjust in a gentle manner.

Can we have more than one soulmate?

It is possible to love more than one spirit in the deep, enduring way of a partner. Hence it is possible to have more than one soulmate.

Despite this, some spirits choose a primary soulmate with whom they have a special affinity and this bond is stronger than other relationships.

> *The mistake is in believing our romantic partners on Earth have to be our soulmates. If we still have lessons to learn with them, we should not expect 'smooth sailing'.*

A life in which we have chosen a great deal of growth may well include a great deal of sacrifice. A soulmate who has contracted to help us may not play the role of the ideal partner in such circumstances.

Does sex exist in the spirit world?

The main evolutionary function of sex is procreation and does not exist in the spirit world. This does not mean we will not have intense vibrations of pleasure when we reconnect with someone special. We most certainly will; however, the vibration is not sexual in a human sense.

> *It is worth mentioning that any obsessive or addictive habit can be difficult to give up as it may remain in the energetic memory of a soul, even after the human's death.*

Hence, some souls need healing for their addictive memories in the spirit world.

Although a soul can use their energy when they cross to the spirit world to create the illusion of a physical life, enjoying old hobbies, eating and drinking if they choose, their desire to maintain physical pleasures eventually wanes. When they are ready, they will continue learning as a spirit of light and begin planning their next incarnation.

What is a soul contract?

A soul contract is a voluntary agreement between spirits that is made before coming to Earth.

It may involve members of your soul group as well as other spirits who are willing to work with you.

Before we reincarnate, we are shown options and probabilities that accompany a range of possible lives. We are able to choose the parents, family and general circumstances we will be born into. Some soul groups make these selections as a team while other groups are less fixed, and individuals move between different groups.

Spirits volunteer to take part in our lives by acting in specific roles so that we are given opportunities to develop the lessons and qualities we need. These might include strength, independence, courage, compassion, service to others, self-confidence, humility and so on. Our spiritual friends might also give us a shake-up, so we are forced to look at where our lives are heading and re- evaluate.

A soul contract is never an excuse for cruelty or abuse. Every spirit has to face their life-review by experiencing the impact of their actions on others.

Our freewill allows us to choose how we will fulfil any soul contract. Cruelty is not the soul's choice, but rather a human weakness of personality or mental illness.

What happens if we do not fulfil our soul contracts?

It is tough being a spirit inside a human body. It is easy to forget why we are here and to deviate from our ideal path.

If we forget our soul contracts or fail to recognize the signals we left for ourselves before our birth, it does not mean our life is a complete failure. Firstly, through our spiritual development and previous experiences on Earth, we may unconsciously make wise decisions. If we become tempted to abuse our power, many of us will know that this is not advisable.

Secondly, there is no cosmic punishment for failing to remember a soul contract or being unable to fulfil it. We are given opportunities across a range of lives to make progress, and it is with loving concern that our evaluation of each life occurs when we return to the spirit world.

What is karma?

Karma is the principle of taking responsibility for our actions and the impacts these actions created. It is a spiritual law and cannot be evaded.

However, karma is not a negative, punishing principle as many believe. Put simply, for each action there is a consequence. In other words, how we choose to use our freewill matters.

> *If our freewill hurts others, then we will have to address the impact of our actions, either in the current life or another.*

If we recognize our mistakes and learn our lessons early enough to make positive changes, then the consequences may be fewer and our life-review more pleasant.

However, given our human natures, it is difficult to avoid accruing karma while we are 'asleep' to our real purpose in incarnating to Earth.

Awaking to our spiritual nature, and offering compassion and love to all beings, including to our self, is one way to minimize accruing karma that needs to be balanced in following lives.

The current Dalai Lama believes that the best way to relieve our own suffering is to be of service to others.

Is the future set before we come to Earth?

Our choices influence our future on a second by second basis.

It is true that some events are fixed on our life-path; however how we respond to these events creates a range of probabilities.

We are born with a karmic blueprint of likely experiences and possible relationships. Many of them were known to us in the spirit world, and members of our soul group contracted to participate in these relationships.

Then amnesia struck us when the soul bonded with the human foetus and the principle of freewill began to operate. The soul is reported to come and go as it wishes during the pregnancy; however, at some point shortly after birth, the bonding becomes long term.

> *Every action we take or decision we make creates probabilities. These probabilities are seen by psychics who may make the mistake of telling you what your future will be.*
>
> *You need to understand that probability is not the same as destiny. You can shape many events by altering your life-decisions.*

The exception is an event that is fixed on your timeline such as a birth, death or other experience to which you have already agreed.

What is synchronicity and why does it happen?

Synchronicity can also be called 'meaningful coincidences'.

> *Synchronicity occurs when two meaningful and similar, but seemingly unrelated events occur simultaneously.*

A stunning example of synchronicity occurred when my daughter asked me to care for her cat during the Christmas period. The cat, whose name is Bandit, had just caught an infection and my daughter emphasized several times how important it was that he be locked in the house for several days. No matter how desperate Bandit was to go outside, I was instructed to keep him in.

The next day my son, who lives four hundred kilometers away, arrived home for Christmas. He presented me with an early Christmas gift. It was a small plaque with a picture of a cat on it. The inscription read, "*Don't let the cat out no matter what it tells you.*"

The synchronicity of these events astounded me. Even more incredible is the fact my son had purchased the plaque from a pharmacy about three days before Bandit became sick. Obviously, the fight that gave Bandit his infected ear was already on his timeline.

Synchronicity can also occur when you think of a person and in that moment, they phone.

In meaningful examples of synchronicity, you are prompted to stop and notice what is occurring.

Often, synchronicity is your spiritual friends' way of showing you that nothing occurs by chance. Your spiritual guidance is urging you to be alert to their contact and watch out for their messages. It can also occur when you recognize a signpost that you put on your timeline before your birth.

How can I communicate with my guides and loved ones?

An energetic bridge must be built before the human and spirit worlds can meet. This is because our friends in the spirit world vibrate at a higher frequency than souls like us who are 'cloaked' in a human body. In order to receive communication from your spiritual friends, you need to raise your vibration.

Meditation and peaceful contemplation are two effective ways to settle emotional disturbances and raise your energy. Lifting your energy is also known as connecting to your spiritual power. Some people find happy activities such as dancing or exercise lift their vibration so they can connect with Spirit. The best technique is what works best for you.

It is important that you understand your spiritual friends are close to you at any time. It is your ability to reach them that is impaired not their ability to support you.

If you would like to know how to make effective connections with Spirit, refer to my book, *'Your Intuitive Gifts At Work. From Passion to Profession. The 8 Keys to Excellence in Spiritual Practice.'*

What are spirit guides and what roles do they play?

Spirit guides have reached a stage of development where they can offer assistance to your soul's growth during human lifetimes. They may also be your teachers and guides while you are in the spirit world.

While family members and friends who have crossed into the spirit world can be your guides, (often called family or familiar guides), your teaching guides will not have incarnated with you in your current life. Your teaching guides have the responsibility for assisting your soul's development.

You may have one or more guides who are with you during your entire lifetime, while others step into your vibration for a period of months or years as you learn particular lessons. Some help you with gifts, such as writing, teaching, music, healing, particular skills and spiritual development. Others help you with life issues, such as relationships, family issues, school or university, self-confidence, work and so on.

The way to communicate with the spirit world is to set a clear intention. If you wish to contact teaching guides, ask for them specifically. If you want to contact a family member or a friend, make it clear. You are in charge of your communication. Remember to express respect and gratitude for any healing energies or messages received.

Do I need to protect myself when I communicate with my spiritual team?

In the same way as you would not open your home to random people passing by, you should not open your energy field, (called your aura), to uninvited spiritual beings.

When you intend spiritual communication, you raise your vibration and also your spiritual light. This is visible to spiritual beings, some of whom may still be having a hard time adjusting to their new circumstances. Unless you are a trained medium, it is always best to communicate only with your loved ones or guides. The thoughts and energy of spirits on the lower astral planes can be confusing. However, the spirit world is one of intelligence; these confused spirits are never abandoned, and help is always at hand when they are ready to accept it.

Setting a clear intention that you will work or communicate with only those beings from the White Light is important. When you affirm that only spiritual beings who are from the Divine Light may approach your vibration, you ensure no beings on the lower astral planes interfere with your efforts to contact your loved ones. While views differ on this, I request protection whenever I make contact with my spiritual team. It is an automatic aspect of my spiritual practice.

Prayer is another powerful means of connecting you with spiritual assistance. I pray frequently and believe prayer is always heard.

Pray to whatever Divine Power you believe in and remember that the Divine Will is the best outcome to seek. We cannot know or understand the Divine Plan and may not know where the Soul's path truly lies.

How do we recognize each other in the spirit world?

As a spirit crosses from a human life into the spirit world it is met by members of their soul family or a teaching guide. Recognition is reported to be instantaneous even if we have not known this guide during our most recent life.

When we incarnate to Earth, some of our energy remains in the spirit world. The *whole you* understands your soul's entire journey - where you have been, where you need to go and who is working with you.

Time only exists in our human dimension. What seems to take a long time for us, is like a crack in the pavement in the spirit world.

In the spirit world there is an 'eternal now'. Your spiritual friends move close to you with the speed of thought and they know when you are ready to re-join them.

Every spirit has its own vibration in color, frequency and sound. You are as much an individual in spirit, as you are on Earth. There is no risk that you will not be recognized or welcomed.

Some spirits need healing and rest if they have suffered prior to passing over. This occurs in designated places in the spirit world. Others are ready to resume their spiritual lives immediately.

A spirit who has inflicted harm on others may need to spend time recovering and readjusting to the spirit world. Their accountability for their actions needs to be thoroughly explored and experienced.

It is also true that some spirits can delay their crossing into the Light at death. They linger in the lower astral planes, which are the closest vibration to our own. This may be because they are unwilling to leave a physical life and are tied to Earthly addictions. The shock of death may also have confused them, or they may believe they need to stay close to Earth to help those they love.

Without doubt, crossing into the Light of the Source to be healed is the option we all need to take. We can do so much more to assist our loved ones once we are strong spiritual beings ourselves.

Special helpers assist confused spirits to cross over, as do many humans through their own spiritual gifts. These examples are exceptions to the standard experience of being drawn into the White Light and met by family members or a guide.

It is important to add that people who take their lives through suicide are greeted with compassion when they enter the spirit world. Sometimes, the struggle of remaining in a human body is just too great. Once in the spirit world, the newly arrived spirit will experience the impacts of their decision on their soul's growth and also on the lives of those left behind. It is likely they will return to complete unfinished lessons in another incarnation when it is appropriate. Many are deeply regretful of the pain their suicide caused the ones they love, but still feel it was the only decision they knew how to make at the time.

How do we communicate with each other in the spirit world?

Communication occurs through telepathy. There is no need to speak; however, you will 'hear' thoughts.

What do we look like, as humans, to spirit?

Spirit seems to have a clear view of us as humans. A loved one may see you looking at their photo, changing the color of paint in your home or planting a certain flower in the garden. This confirms they can see our world as it is.

Do I grow old in the spirit world?

Aging, as we know it, does not exist in the spirit world. When we cross over, we can choose an age from a recent life we would like to be. For example, a parent who is providing a message for a child will show the medium an image of themselves that the child can relate to. Children who have died may reveal themselves to their parents at the age they passed, and then show themselves at an age they would be if still living now. This helps the parents validate they are speaking to the spirit of their child.

The age of a spirit is not measured by its human years. Children on Earth can be very old souls, and some choose to exit life early for reasons only they, their guides and their soul family know.

What happens if I've had more than one spouse? Will that cause problems?

As soon as we readjust to the spirit world, we remember who we are and the members of our soul family.

Clients who have undergone spiritual regression through hypnotherapy report the spirit world is a place of understanding and love. The human jealousies we have on Earth are no longer relevant. We will spend time with the spirits we feel connected to within our soul group. We will not remain close to spirits with whom we need no further relationship.

Is a soul the same as a spirit?

Many people ask if a soul and a spirit are the same. While some use these terms interchangeably, there is a difference. The soul exists while we continue to reincarnate. It houses our Divine spark which is pure spirit. Our spirit lives within the vessel of the soul.

Our soul records all our experiences and lessons. It helps us make the transitions from Earth to the spirit world, and back to Earth again when we are reborn. We often talk about 'souls on board' when lives are lost. This acknowledges the spiritual aspect of humankind. Eventually, when we are able to blend in unconditional love with the Divine Source, we will become pure spirit and the need for the soul will disappear.

If you hold any interest in the Holy Bible, it distinguishes between the body, soul and spirit as three separate entities. However, people often use the two without understanding the subtle differences, and this does not matter in most circumstances.

ACKNOWLEDGEMENTS

Gratitude

My sincere thanks to John Noble, who has graciously allowed me to share many cameo-moments from our relationship in this book. Our karmic journey continues as husband and wife.

Dedication

This book is dedicated to the memory of my soul-sister and childhood friend, Kerri-Anne, who taught me to love life and seize opportunities for joy. Kerri-Anne left her Earthly life suddenly, but she has inspired this book from the spirit world.

TESTIMONIALS

"*Karma Couples* is very helpful, down to earth and practical with strategies to negotiate problem relationships, culminating in Standing up for your Truth. It's well-written and easily understood."

Gail Ahlstrom

"Michelle has been guiding our group with many different aspects of Intuitive Development including Psychic Development, Connecting with our Guides, Soul Readings, Mediumship, Card Reading, Spiritual Healing and Trance, just to name a few. I have also have recently joined Michelle's Online Live teaching sessions, which are most informative and interactive.

Michelle is very passionate with her teaching and shares this with much love and enthusiasm. Her style is very informative yet simple enough for us to understand. There's lots of practical work, which we love. Michelle is a fabulous, innovative teacher and we all feel very blessed to be part of her group."

Wendy Lee

TESTIMONIALS

"Michelle Robinson is a treasure. She operates from a heart filled with love, compassion and much wisdom. I have found her teaching to be very informative, fun yet serious, and well organised and delivered. I'm grateful for the opportunities I've had to share these experiences and to further my own personal growth."

Pauline Wearne

"I feel very blessed to have met Michelle. She is very gifted, yet humble. Her willingness to share her knowledge and experiences is commendable. Michelle gives so much. People walk away from her workshops feeling happy and inspired."

Pam Turner

MEET THE AUTHOR

Michelle Robinson

B.A., Dip. Ed, B. Counseling, Dip. Clinical Hypnosis, Cert. Soul Regression

Michelle comes from a mainstream background; however, using her intuitive gifts is both her passion and profession. She is a qualified teacher, counselor and hypnotherapist with twenty years' experience working with adults and teenagers.

Michelle has studied extensively with Australian and international Mediums, Psychics and Healers. She facilitates groups and provides one on one and group online mentoring.

Topics include Inspired Trance, Trance Healing, Reiki, Development of Psychic and Mediumship Skills, Past Life Exploration and Personal Empowerment. She has a practical approach to spirituality, knowing it is important to stay grounded and authentic. Trance is one of her special gifts, and she receives channelled wisdom from a team of spiritual guides.

Michelle is a published author of books and Oracle Cards.

These works include:

I'm Positive! Program
Your Thoughts and
Feelings to Create a
Positive Life.

**Your Intuitive
Gifts At Work**
From Passion to
Profession. The 8 Keys
to Excellence in Spiritual
Practice.

Karma Couples
A Spiritual Self-Help
Guide for Troubled
Karmic Relationships.

Daily Compass Oracle Cards
Guidance for Everyday Life
A 53 Card Deck and Guidebook

Open to Spirit Oracle Cards
Embrace the Wisdom of Spirit
A 50 Card Deck and
Guidebook

In 2019 Michelle and husband, John Noble established **The Academy of Spiritual Practice.**

She launched her first of many online courses:
Certificate in Advanced Spiritual Practice

The Academy's vision is to share the inspiration of Spirit by offering Michelle's spiritual development programs and authored works online.

Email Michelle: michelle@academyofspiritualpractice.com to learn more about mentoring and training opportunities.

Websites:
www.trustyourintuition.com
www.academyofspiritualpractice.com

Contact:
michelle@academyofspiritualpractice.com

OTHER BOOKS AND PRODUCTS BY MICHELLE ROBINSON

Your Intuitive Gifts At Work will propel you toward excellence in working with your intuitive gifts
Inside you will find 8 Master Keys.

These Keys reveal how to fine-tune your skills and master your spiritual connections so that your gifts reach their full potential. The keys give you the structure and guidance to transform your passion to your profession. Whether you help others as a psychic, a medium, a healer or in any aligned field, understanding the principles and steps required to launch an inspired Intuitive Practice sets you on the road to success.

Available from www.trustyourintuition.com/shop-now
Contact Michelle: michelle@academyofspiritualpractice.com for information about her online teaching program developed from this book.

I'm Positive! helps you let go of unhelpful thought patterns, emotional hurt and outdated beliefs so you feel confident, optimistic and in control of your choices. If you have been undermining your own achievements or impacted by the negativity of others, this book shows you how to steer your life in the right direction.

Program your mind so that positive thoughts and feelings are your natural default.

This book includes access to 6 complimentary guided MP3 audios to guide you through the activities from the book.

Available from www.trustyourintuition.com/shop-now

STUDY ONLINE WITH BY MICHELLE ROBINSON

The Certificate in Advanced Intuitive Practice

This flexibly delivered, 9 module online program helps you propel your intuitive gifts to their highest potential. Eight Keys to Excellence guide you towards establishing best practice in using your intuitive gifts, whether you work with psychic skills, evidential mediumship, trance mediumship or spiritual healing.

You will learn strategies to create the confidence and courage to step up and work with your gifts. If using your intuitive gifts is your passion, you will receive the skills and knowledge to transform that passion into your profession. During this program you will connect with your soul's calling and develop closer relationships with your spiritual guides. You will also receive practical strategies and tips to guide you to set up and market your own intuitive practice. This program helps you find the balance between living a human life, which is important, and fulfilling your soul's reasons for incarnating in this life.

Email Michelle for more information:
michelle@academyofspiritualpractice.com

Enrol Now:
https://www.yourintuitivegiftsatwork.com/advancedcourse

Or go to www.trustyourintuiton.com/shop-now

CARD DECKS BY MICHELLE ROBINSON

Daily Compass Oracle Cards

This deck unites the wisdom of Spirit with positive messages for everyday life.

I have worked with thousands of people whose lack of self-confidence sabotages them from living their best lives. They feel too anxious or unworthy to find the happiness they deserve. Yet, when communicating with Spirit, I am consistently in awe of the great love and encouragement our Spiritual Guides and Loved Ones offer us. They never want us to give up on ourselves. Their encouragement is conveyed in these cards.

The 'Daily Compass' helps you navigate your life with greater clarity and confidence. The cards are uplifting and practical, suitable for all levels of experience.
www.trustyourintuition.com/shop-now

Open to Spirit Oracle Cards

This stunning deck offers insights of encouragement and hope. It's beautiful imagery and messages take you on an inward journey, away from the hectic physical world.

Many people live busy and ungrounded lives. Their mind is so overwhelmed that their Soul feels unheard amid the demands of daily life. This deck listens to the calling of your Soul. It provides gentle spiritual nourishment, offering wisdom that is deeper than a standard, psychic message.

Whether your chosen cards provide insights about your intuitive gifts, your soul's calling, self-healing or messages from the Spirit World, you will feel uplifted, supported and loved.

www.trustyourintuition.com/shop-now

www.ingramcontent.com/pod-product-compliance
Lightning Source LLC
Chambersburg PA
CBHW070108120526
44588CB00032B/1387